Essential Events

The Capture and Killing of

Osama bin Laden

Essential Events

THE CAPTURE AND KILLING OF
OSAMA BIN LADEN

BY MARCIA AMIDON LUSTED

ABDO
Publishing Company

Content Consultant
David C. Rapoport
Professor Emeritus, Political Science University of California,
Los Angeles, Founding Editor, *Terrorism and Political Violence*

CREDITS

Published by ABDO Publishing Company, 8000 West 78th Street, Edina, Minnesota 55439. Copyright © 2012 by Abdo Consulting Group, Inc. International copyrights reserved in all countries. No part of this book may be reproduced in any form without written permission from the publisher. The Essential Library™ is a trademark and logo of ABDO Publishing Company.

Printed in the United States of America,
North Mankato, Minnesota
082011
122011

♻ THIS BOOK CONTAINS AT LEAST 10% RECYCLED MATERIALS.

Editor: Melissa York
Copy Editor: Mary Jo Platt
Cover Design: Becky Daum
Interior Design and Production: Kazuko Collins

Library of Congress Cataloging-in-Publication Data
Lusted, Marcia Amidon.
   The capture and killing of Osama bin Laden / by Marcia Amidon Lusted.
      p. cm. -- (Essential events)
   Includes bibliographical references and index.
   ISBN 978-1-61783-180-5
   1. Bin Laden, Osama, 1957-2011--Juvenile literature.
2. Terrorists--Biography--Juvenile literature. 3. Qaida (Organization)--Juvenile literature. 4. Terrorism--Juvenile literature. 5. Terrorism--United States--Juvenile literature. 6. Terrorism--United States--Prevention--Juvenile literature. I. Title.
   HV6430.B55L87 2012
   958.104'7092--dc23
                                              2011025479

The Capture and Killing
of Osama bin Laden

TABLE OF CONTENTS

*The September 11, 2001, terror attacks destroyed
the World Trade Center in New York City.*

SEPTEMBER 11, 2001

I t was a Tuesday morning in September
that seemed no different from other
mornings. People went to work and kids went to
school. Life for most people in the United States was
normal. But this day, September 11, 2001, would

become a day that most people would never forget. It was a day that, 20 or 50 years later, people will still know exactly what they were doing when they heard the news.

A Chain of Tragedies

At approximately 8:00 a.m., an airplane left Logan Airport in Boston, Massachusetts. United Airlines (UA) flight 175 was a routine flight headed for Los Angeles, California. A few minutes later, American Airlines (AA) flight 11 left Boston and also headed for Los Angeles. AA flight 77 left Dulles Airport outside Washington, DC, at 8:21 a.m., headed for Los Angeles as well. And at approximately 8:40 a.m., UA flight 93 left Newark, New Jersey, headed for San Francisco, California. But none of these flights would ever reach its intended destination. Terrorists seized control of all four flights. At 8:46 a.m., AA flight 11 crashed into the North Tower of the World Trade Center's twin tower skyscrapers in New York City. At 9:03 a.m., UA flight 175 crashed into the South Tower of the World Trade Center. At 9:59 a.m., the South Tower collapsed, followed by the North Tower at 10:28 a.m., killing many who worked inside as well as people who had gone in to help those injured or trapped in the initial attacks.

Meanwhile, AA flight 77 crashed into the Pentagon in Washington DC. The fourth flight, UA flight 93, crashed near Shanksville, Pennsylvania. It is believed UA flight 93 was on a flight path toward the White House or the US Capitol building.

Americans watched in horror and disbelief as it became apparent that these crashes were the work of terrorists. They had targeted symbols

---

Flight 93

United Airlines (UA) flight 93 left Newark, New Jersey, and experts believe it was intended to crash into the White House or the US Capitol. However, it crashed into a farm field in Shanksville, Pennsylvania. It was the heroic actions of the passengers and crew onboard flight 93 that prevented another attack on a US symbol. When the hijackers took control of the flight, passengers and crew members used the air phones on the plane to report the hijacking. Then they learned about the other flights that had crashed that morning. Realizing that the same thing was intended for their flight, they voted to fight back.

The cockpit voice recorder captured the sounds of their struggle: shouts, screams, calls to action, and sounds of breaking glassware. To stop the uprising, the terrorist piloting the aircraft began to roll it to the left and right, and pitch the nose up and down. In its final moments, the plane turned upside down. . . . The terrorists chose to crash [the plane] rather than risk the passengers and crew regaining control of the aircraft.[1]

Forty civilians and four hijackers died when the airplane crashed. There were no survivors. But because of the courage of the people on board, UA flight 93 was the only flight that did not carry out its terrorist attack.

of the United States, buildings that represented the country's power, economy, and government. As Roger Simon said in an article in *U.S. News and World Report* a few days after the attacks:

> *Life as we know it in these United States ended Tuesday morning. In the place where the World Trade Center once stood, black smoke billowed against a heart-breakingly blue sky. All who saw it knew immediately that . . . we would never again feel completely safe.*[2]

Some 3,000 people lost their lives in the airplanes and on the ground that Tuesday, which would forever be remembered as 9/11. President George W. Bush stated that the United States had suffered "an apparent terrorist attack" and promised to "hunt down and find those folks who committed this act."[3] For the first time in US history, the Federal Aviation Administration grounded all flights in the United States. Government buildings were evacuated and all US financial markets were closed. Everyday life in the United States came to a halt. People were left wondering if this was just the beginning of an all-out terrorist war.

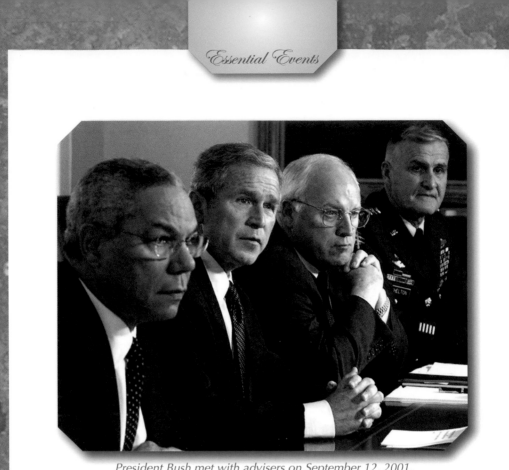

President Bush met with advisers on September 12, 2001.
From left: *Secretary of State Colin Powell, President Bush,*
Vice President Dick Cheney, General Henry Shelton

WHO WAS TO BLAME?

Immediately following the 9/11 attacks, Americans and the US government began seeking the perpetrators of these acts of terrorism. It was not long before the government began scrutinizing a network of Islamic terrorists known as al-Qaeda and its leader, Osama bin Laden. He had been placed on the Most Wanted Terrorists list put out by the Federal Bureau of Investigation (FBI) in 1999.

His men had previously boasted they were planning to carry out an unprecedented attack on the United States. They had already claimed responsibility for the 1998 bombing of two US embassies in Africa, as well as an attack on a US warship, the USS *Cole*, in 2000. The planning and coordination necessary to carry out the 9/11 attacks pointed to al-Qaeda. Bin Laden initially denied having anything to do with the attacks, saying, "I stress that I have not carried out this act."[4] Eventually, however, he would be heard on a videotaped interview claiming responsibility, saying, "We calculated in advance the number of casualties."[5]

Bin Laden was now the face of the tragedy of 9/11. Many feared this was just a small part of what bin Laden and his organization could do.

The United States was determined to hunt down bin Laden and bring him to justice.

Fast Forward

Nearly ten years passed. Despite many attempts, the US government and the Central Intelligence Agency

Ground Zero

Ground Zero is the term used for the former location of the World Trade Center, which was demolished after the 9/11 attacks. The term itself is a description of a place where a nuclear bomb had exploded. A memorial to the victims of the attack was set to open at Ground Zero on September 12, 2011.

(CIA) had not captured or found bin Laden. Little had been discovered about his whereabouts. Then, in a press conference on May 2, 2011, President Barack Obama made the following announcement:

> *Good evening. Tonight, I can report to the American people and to the world that the United States has conducted an operation that killed Osama bin Laden.*[6]

The man whom most Americans thought of as their number one public enemy was dead, and his body was sunk to the bottom of the Arabian Sea. But the journey that led from his rise as a terrorist, through the events of 9/11, and to his death in Pakistan in 2011 was a long one. Who was Osama bin Laden, and what had made him who he was, one of the most recognizable terrorists in the world?

The Patriot Act

On October 26, 2001, President George W. Bush signed into law the USA PATRIOT Act. Its name is an acronym that stands for Uniting and Strengthening America by Providing Appropriate Tools Required to Intercept and Obstruct Terrorism. This act gave law enforcement officials greater ability to search telephone, e-mail, medical, financial, and other records. It also expanded the definition of terrorism. The updated definition granted US officials more power to investigate possible terrorist activities within the country.

بن لادن

تنظيم القاعدة

*Osama bin Laden praised God for the September 11 attacks in a video
that aired on television on October 7, 2001.*

*Ruins of Alamut Castle in Iran, a stronghold
of the Islamic terrorist group the Assassins*

A History of Terrorism

Terrorism is defined as the use of violence
and threats to intimidate or coerce,
especially for political reasons. For thousands of
years, rebels and governments have used terrorist
tactics to control civilians or influence politics.

THE FIRST TERRORISTS

The earliest recorded group of terrorists was active during the first century CE, 2,000 years ago. This group was known as the Zealots of Judea, though the Romans called them *sicarii*, or "dagger men." They used terrorist tactics against the Romans who occupied their homeland of Judea and Jewish people who collaborated with the Romans. From the eleventh to the thirteenth century CE, a group of Islamic terrorists called the Assassins was active. Their intent was to purify Islam. They killed Islamic leaders whom they felt allowed the corruption of Islam. The words *assassin* and *assassinate* come from this group's name. Both of these groups used terrorist tactics to achieve their ends, and both based their activities on religious motivations.

From the fourteenth to the eighteenth century, terrorism became less common as conventional war and conflict increased. The causes that had inspired terrorist behavior in earlier times, such as religious conflicts or conflicts between different ethnic groups, usually led to all-out war. It was not until small warring kingdoms and states evolved into larger, more established nations that terrorism became common again.

The French Reign of Terror was notorious for its executions by guillotine.

THE FRENCH REVOLUTION

The words *terrorism* and *terrorist* were not used until the time of the French Revolution, when the French revolutionary government used a system called the Reign of Terror during 1793 and 1794. The term *terrorist* was employed against those considered to be the revolution's enemies. After the Reign of Terror, terrorism was no longer something limited to revolutionary groups and religious sects. It also became a tool of governments.

By the nineteenth century, terrorism was on the rise. Rebels found that terrorist acts also could be thought of as heroic and noble efforts to liberate the oppressed. For this reason, terrorist tactics became very popular with anarchist groups who wanted to change their governments. Small groups of revolutionaries used terrorist tactics to attack governments. The 1890s are often referred to as the "Golden Age of Assassination," as monarchs, presidents, and prime ministers were assassinated in rapid succession. Heads of state in Russia, France, Spain, the United States, and other countries were assassinated by small groups of people opposed to their governments. In Russia, a small group of revolutionaries known as "The People's Will" protested the czarist government and ultimately led to the assassination of Czar Alexander II and his family in 1881.

Dynamite

Dynamite was invented in 1860. It was intended to make mining easier, but was soon adopted by terrorist groups for making bombs. A single person can use a bomb to injure or kill many people at the same time. Before the invention of dynamite, a terrorist group needed to gather a mob of people to cause large-scale destruction.

These groups were generally not well organized. They typically refused to work with other groups and therefore did not become large-scale political groups. However, improvements in mass communications and transportation such as the telegraph and the railroad allowed terrorists to coordinate with like-minded associates in different countries. This was the first time groups in different countries were moved by the same concerns and acted together in any way.

Another trend emerging during this time was nationalism. Governments began combining their citizens' personal identities with the national identity of their government or

Four Waves of Terrorism

Many scholars understand modern terrorism to consist of four waves or broad movements. Modern terrorism is different from what came before because it involves groups in different countries acting together in some ways. The first wave was anarchist and included the political assassinations of the late nineteenth and early twentieth centuries. The second wave began in the 1920s and included revolts against colonial powers such as the United Kingdom and the United States by people in dependent territories. The third wave began in the 1960s and began as a reaction to the Vietnam War, which reached its height between 1963 and 1973. Third-wave terrorists hijacked airplanes to take hostages and make ransom demands. Terrorists of the fourth wave are motivated by religious concerns. Many of these terrorist groups want to replace secular governments with religious ones. Islam is at the center of this movement, but all religions have produced terrorist groups during this time. Scholars generally date the fourth wave to 1979.

nation. Those citizens who did not want to give up their individuality or religion were left with few options and sometimes turned to terrorist tactics. An example of this was the struggle of the Irish people to maintain their own country and identity separate from the United Kingdom. This struggle led to many terrorist activities during the twentieth century.

By the end of the twentieth century and the beginning of the twenty-first, terrorism was a growing issue all over the world. In 1992, the United Nations defined terrorism as:

> An anxiety-inspiring method of repeated violent action, employed by (semi-) clandestine individual, group or state actors, for idiosyncratic, criminal or political reasons, whereby—in contrast to assassination—the direct targets of violence are not the main targets.[1]

TERRORISM IN THE UNITED STATES

In the United States, terrorism had been used domestically since the Civil War. White supremacist

William McKinley

On September 16, 1901, President William McKinley was assassinated by Leon Czolgosz during a visit to the Pan-American Exposition in New York. Czolgosz, an anarchist, believed that government was evil and said, "I killed President McKinley because I done my duty. I didn't believe one man should have so much service and another man should have none."[2]

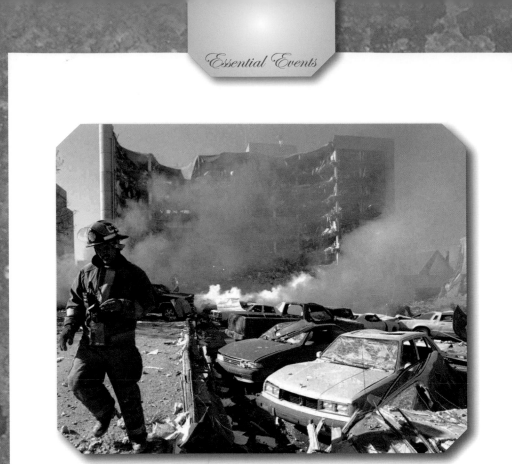

A firefighter walks away from the Alfred P. Murrah Federal Building in Oklahoma City, Oklahoma, in the aftermath of the 1995 bombing.

groups such as the Ku Klux Klan used terrorist tactics against African Americans and those sympathetic to their cause. During the 1920s, when capitalism was making some people wildly rich, anarchists and communists protested against the inequality of rich and poor. On September 16, 1920, an explosion across the street from the J. P. Morgan bank headquarters on Wall Street in New York City ripped through the building.

The explosion killed 30 people and injured hundreds more. While those responsible were never caught, a group called the American Anarchist Fighters claimed credit.

This Wall Street bombing was the deadliest US terrorism attack until April 19, 1995, when an explosion destroyed the Alfred P. Murrah Federal Building in Oklahoma City, Oklahoma. There were 168 deaths and more than 600 injuries. Members of a pro-militia group launched the attack as a protest against the government by detonating a truck filled with explosives.

As a result of this attack, federal buildings and other government facilities tightened security. The Oklahoma City bombing would be the most shocking terrorist act in the United States until the 9/11 attacks in 2001. It was one of the first wake-up calls that terrorism was a very real threat to everyone, everywhere.

Baylee Almon

The image of an infant rescued from the day care center in the rubble of the destroyed federal building has come to represent the tragedy of the Oklahoma City bombing. Baylee Almon was only one year old when firefighter Chris Fields carried her out of the ruins. She later died at a local hospital. Charles Porter's photograph of the incident won a 1996 Pulitzer Prize.

Complacency

Before the Oklahoma City bombing, and even up until the 9/11 attacks, most Americans viewed terrorism as something that happened somewhere else. Many European countries had experienced large acts of modern terrorism and were more concerned with security. Americans, however, had never experienced precautions such as intensive screenings at airports or in-depth searches at borders. Before the increase in hijacking attempts in the late 1960s and early 1970s, airport security was loose. It was not until the hijacking of four airplanes by Palestinian terrorists in September 1970 that President Richard Nixon ordered sky marshals on select flights. Other new measures included passenger and baggage screening before boarding and the use of metal detectors. Still, until 9/11, most Americans falsely believed terrorism had rarely occurred within their country's borders and thought they did not need to worry about it. It would take Osama bin Laden to make them aware of how vulnerable they really were. According to author Adam Roberts:

The attacks on the World Trade Center and the Pentagon on September 11 confirmed that terrorism had acquired a new face. Terrorists were now engaged in a campaign of suicide and mass murder on a huge scale. Previously it had been possible to believe that there were limits beyond which even terrorists would not go. After the thousands of deaths on September 11, it was evident that at least one group would stop at nothing.[3]

HOLY WAR

Modern Islamic terrorism, which culminated in the 9/11 attacks, began to take shape through several key events in 1979. Religion was becoming a more powerful force for uniting people than the nationalist identities that were important in the earlier twentieth century. A revolution in Iran replaced a secular government with an Islamic state. The strong religious government in Iran encouraged similar uprisings and acts of terrorism in other Middle Eastern countries.

World Trade Center 1993

The 2001 attacks that destroyed the World Trade Center were not the first terrorist acts to take place there. On February 26, 1993, a bomb carried by a truck detonated underneath the North Tower. It was intended to destroy both towers, but failed to do so, although it did kill six people and injure many more. According to the FBI:

A thunderous explosion rocked lower Manhattan. The epicenter was the parking garage beneath the World Trade Center, where a massive eruption carved out a nearly 100-foot crater several stories deep and several more high. Six people were killed almost instantly. . . . More than a thousand people were hurt in some way, some badly, with crushed limbs.[4]

A group of Arabic conspirators were charged with the bombing, but it is not known exactly for whom they were working or if they had ties to Osama bin Laden.

"Islamic groups have conducted the most significant, deadly, and [profound] international attacks . . . and the successes achieved apparently influenced religious terror groups elsewhere."[5]

—*Professor David C. Rapoport*

In the meantime, the Soviet Union invaded Afghanistan. This attack pushed Muslims from around the world into jihad, or holy war, to regain the Muslim-majority country from the secular Soviets. The United States provided weapons and aid to the Afghans and their allies, helping force out the Soviets by 1989. This war proved to terrorist organizations that small religious groups could defeat a superpower. It also left them equipped with modern weapons and effective guerrilla warfare tactics. Islamic forces from the Afghan conflict moved into other Muslim-majority regions in the Soviet Union, sparking rebellions that contributed to the country's disintegration. With the Soviet Union brought to its knees, the Islamic terrorist groups were becoming ready to take on the world's last remaining superpower: the United States. Their goals would be to destroy US targets and to force the United States to remove its military entirely from Islamic nations.

Afghan rebels during the Soviet invasion of Afghanistan, February 1980

Osama bin Laden spent much of his youth in Jidda, Saudi Arabia, on the shore of the Red Sea.

WHO WAS OSAMA BIN LADEN?

*I*t is difficult to find out much about Osama bin Laden's childhood, and many of the sources of information about him are unreliable. He was born on March 10, 1957, in Riyadh, the capital of Saudi Arabia. His Syrian mother, Alia Ghanem, was the tenth wife of his father, Mohammad bin Awad bin Laden. Osama was their only child, but Osama is said to have been the seventh son among 50 half brothers and sisters. Sources disagree on the details of Osama's childhood. Some mention that his mother and father divorced, and that his mother remarried and had more children. Others mention no divorce. It is unclear if his parents divorced whether Osama lived with his natural father or his stepfather. His natural father died when Osama was between the ages of five and 15. At some point during his childhood, Osama's family moved to Jidda, Saudi Arabia.

A Religious Life

From a very early age, Osama was a devout Muslim. According to an article in *Time* magazine:

> *Khaled Batarfi, a soccer-playing buddy of bin Laden's on the streets of [Jidda], Saudi Arabia, where they both grew up, remembers his solemn friend praying seven times a day (two more than mandated by Islamic convention) and fasting twice a week in imitation of the Prophet Muhammad. For entertainment, bin Laden would assemble a group of friends at his house to chant songs about the liberation of Palestine.*[1]

His natural father worked as a building contractor, and his projects included renovating Islamic holy sites in Mecca and Medina in Saudi Arabia. This made the family extremely wealthy. It also made Osama feel as if he had a direct connection to the two holiest places in Islam. It is said that Osama's father hosted hundreds of pilgrims in his home during the hajj season, which is when Muslim pilgrims make their way to Mecca. The pilgrimage is a religious duty required of every Muslim at least once during his or her lifetime. The hajj season takes place during the twelfth and last month of the Islamic calendar.

Mecca and Medina

The cities of Mecca and Medina are both holy to Muslims. Mecca, located in Saudi Arabia, is the site of the Kaaba mosque. This mosque is believed to be the first place created on Earth and the place where heavenly bliss touches Earth directly. It is said to have been built by Abraham and his son Ishmael. It is covered with gold-embroidered black fabric. All Muslims are directed to pray in the direction of the Kaaba mosque five times a day, no matter where they are in the world. In addition, as part of the Five Pillars of Islam, the five basic acts that are required of all Muslims, Muslims who can afford to are required to make a pilgrimage to Mecca at least once in their lives. Non-Muslims are forbidden from entering Mecca.

Medina, or the "City of the Prophet," is located in western Saudi Arabia. It is the second most holy place in Islam. Muhammad is said to have fled to Medina when he was driven out of Mecca, and there he gathered his first followers. Medina is the location of the Mosque of the Prophet, which was built on the site of Muhammad's home and contains his tomb.

Some of these pilgrims were Islamic leaders and scholars. Sources that presume Osama lived with his natural father imply that Osama felt their influence and formed relationships with some of them. However, since Osama was so young when his father died, this story may not be true.

Osama attended school at Al Thagher Model School, a prestigious high school in Jidda. One of his teachers, Seamus O'Brien, remembered him as "a nice fellow and a good student. There were no problems with him. . . . He was a quiet lad. I suppose silent waters run deep."[2] Many of the students at Al Thagher were members of the Saudi royal family or came from wealthy families. Soon Osama joined an after-school Islamic study group and formed some close friendships. At this point he was well liked, according to an unnamed former classmate:

> *Osama was an honorable student. He kept to himself, but he was honest. If you brought a sandwich to school, people would often steal it as a joke or eat it if you left it on the desk. This was a common thing. We used to leave our valuables with Osama, because he never cheated. He was sober, serious. He didn't cheat or copy from others, but he didn't hide his paper, either, if others wanted to look over his shoulder.[3]*

Many of the teachers at Al Thagher were members of dissident Islamic groups and some had been influenced by a group called the Muslim Brotherhood. One of the group's purposes was to replace secular Arab leaders with Islamic governments, and they were also known to have supported terrorism. One of these brotherhood teachers ran the after-school group that Osama joined. According to reporter Steve Coll, "The teachers often introduced their students more informally to the brotherhood's precepts of Islamic activism, political consciousness, and violent jihad against Christian occupiers or secular leaders."[4] Many people believe that Osama may have gotten his first ideas about violent jihads and other types of political activism from this after-school group.

Islam or Muslim?

What is the difference between the words *Islam* and *Muslim*? Islam is the word that describes the religion itself. A person who follows the Islamic religion is referred to as a Muslim.

It is also reported that Osama first married at the age of 17. In total, sources estimate he had five or six wives and more than 20 children.

University and Beyond

Bin Laden attended King Abdulaziz University in Jidda, majoring in economics and business

Abdullah Azzam died in 1989, leaving Osama bin Laden in complete control of al-Qaeda.

administration. According to *Time* magazine, this is where bin Laden met Islamic studies professor Abdullah Azzam. Azzam traveled to Pakistan after the Soviet Union's invasion of Afghanistan in 1979. Bin Laden followed him there after graduating from college to help defend the mujahideen—the people engaged in jihad. From Pakistan, they planned and gathered supplies for the guerrilla actions they carried out in Afghanistan.

It was during the fighting in Afghanistan that the idea to form a permanent mujahideen group to fight in a global jihad was most likely born. Azzam and bin Laden continued to offer assistance, including money and weapons, to jihad fighters all through the Arab world. Much of it was funded by bin Laden's own personal fortune inherited from his father, rumored to be about $30 million.

The Soviet Union pulled out of Afghanistan in 1989, but Azzam and bin Laden decided to keep their organization alive. They created a base or headquarters for future jihads, and that is how al-Qaeda, or "the base," was named. Bin Laden soon realized that his goals for the organization were different from Azzam's. Azzam wanted to continue fighting for an Islamic government in Afghanistan, but bin Laden wanted al-Qaeda to be ready to fight anywhere in the world. Azzam was killed later in 1989, leaving bin Laden in full control of al-Qaeda. His control over the group was absolute: members swore allegiance to him personally and had to ask permission to speak in his presence. Convinced that God was telling him what to do, bin Laden allowed no advice from al-Qaeda members or his family to redirect his course.

When Iraq, under Saddam Hussein, invaded Kuwait in August 1990, bin Laden met with Saudi Arabia's King Faud and his defense minister. The United States under President George H. W. Bush had sent troops to Saudi Arabia. The troops were supposed to protect Saudi Arabia from the aggressive Iraqis, but the Saudis were wary of the US troops. Bin Laden warned King Faud not to rely on assistance from the US military. He offered to defend Saudi Arabia using his mujahideen group, but the king rejected his offer. Bin Laden then criticized Saudi Arabia, saying that the presence of US troops there was profaning sacred soil. The king expelled bin Laden from Saudi Arabia in 1991.

Bin Laden moved to Sudan, taking the headquarters of al-Qaeda with him. Here he would begin making plans for a huge jihad against the west and the United States.

The bin Laden Family's Wealth

Osama's father, Mohammad bin Laden, had more than 50 children with his various wives. At the time of Mohammad bin Laden's death, his family was rumored to be worth more than $16 billion. When he died, his son Salem bin Laden became head of the family and reorganized the family construction business into the Saudi Binladin Group. Salem was in charge of distributing the family money among his siblings and half siblings. Osama himself received $80 million when his father died, much of which he used to finance terrorist activities. Today Saudi Binladin Group has an estimated worth of $5 billion.

True or Not?

One of the challenges in learning about bin Laden's life is finding sources that are truthful. Because of bin Laden's stature and position among his followers, many stories of his life are intended to glorify his reputation and may not be accurate.

The Public Broadcasting Service (PBS) television show *Frontline* produced a show about bin Laden. They include a biography of him, but caution the reader that it may not be accurate:

"This document was given to FRONTLINE by a source close to bin Laden. . . . FRONTLINE found it a very useful source of information, but could not independently verify much of the information contained herein. Some of the information is true. However, some of it runs contrary to accounts given by other reliable sources. That said, this document does provide some important details regarding bin Laden and his family life."[5]

Because of his outspoken criticism of the presence of US forces, as well as his support of violent jihads and his involvement in them, bin Laden was formally exiled from his home country of Saudi Arabia in 1994. He had repeatedly spoken out against the Saudi government for allowing the presence of US troops there. He ultimately lost his citizenship and was disowned by his family. Some evidence suggests that family members continued to aid bin Laden financially, though nothing has been proven. ⌐

*By the 1990s, bin Laden had begun his jihad
against the United States and the West.*

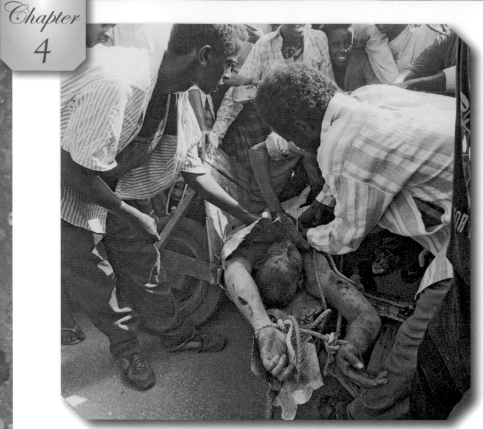

*This US airman was taken from his downed Black Hawk
helicopter in Somalia in 1993 and killed by the crowd.
Bin Laden was linked to the attack.*

DEFENDER OF ISLAM

From his new al-Qaeda headquarters in Sudan, bin Laden coordinated with other radical Islamic groups from the Middle East and North Africa. He set up training camps and business operations. He was planning his jihad against the West.

FATWAS AND ATTACKS

Bin Laden started by issuing a fatwa against the US occupation of Somalia. Bin Laden believed it was his duty to defend Islam against the West, Christianity, and anyone he thought was trying to replace Islamic governments. Bin Laden would follow this with several attacks against US interests. These attacks included his possible involvement in a bombing that damaged part of the World Trade Center in February 1993 (resulting in six deaths and more than 1,000 injured), the downing of two Black Hawk helicopters in Somalia in October 1993 (killing 18 US servicemen), and a 1996 car bomb that exploded outside a US training facility in Khobar, Saudi Arabia, that was being used to train the Saudi Arabian National Guard (killing 19 US servicemen).

Facing international pressure, Sudan forced bin Laden to return to Afghanistan in 1996. There, bin Laden rebuilt al-Qaeda with the help of an Islamic militia group, the Taliban. Now confident that his organization was stronger than ever, bin Laden issued another fatwa against the United States. Published in August 1996, it read in part:

My Muslim Brothers of The World:

Your brothers in Palestine and in the land of the two Holy Places are calling upon your help and asking you to take part in fighting against the enemy—your enemy and their enemy—the Americans and the Israelis. They are asking you to do whatever you can, with one [sic] own means and ability, to expel the enemy, humiliated and defeated, out of the sanctities of Islam.[1]

By 1998, al-Qaeda had merged with the Egyptian Islamic Jihad, making al-Qaeda the headquarters for international terrorism.

In February 1998, bin Laden, along with Ayman al-Zawahiri of the Egyptian Islamic Jihad, issued another fatwa, this one even more specifically targeting Americans. Al-Zawahiri is thought to have actually written the fatwa, but it was issued jointly. It was published in an Arabic language newspaper:

The Taliban

The Taliban gets its name from *taleb*, the Arabic word for "student." Members consider forms of government such as democracy or secular government to be an offense against Islam. They wanted to establish a government that does not tolerate versions of Islam different from their own. The Taliban did successfully establish this kind of government in Afghanistan, which the United States destroyed after 9/11. Today the group operates in northwest Pakistan and in Afghanistan.

*We—with God's help—call on every Muslim who believes in
God and wishes to be rewarded to comply with God's order
to kill the Americans and plunder their money wherever and
whenever they find it.*[2]

THE ATTACKS CONTINUE

Al-Qaeda
carried out even
more attacks
following the fatwa.
In August, US
embassies in Kenya
and Tanzania were
bombed. Trucks
filled with bombs
were driven into
the embassies,
and 220 people
were killed. In
retaliation, the
United States
conducted air
strikes against
several alleged

Jihads

Jihad is a religious duty, something Muslims
must carry out. In some cases it is called
the Sixth Pillar of Islam. Although the word
itself simply means "struggle," it has come
to represent a holy war to defend Islam. It is
a misunderstood term, as most Westerners
now associate it with violence. The struggle
can be an internal one to maintain faith, or a
struggle to improve Islamic society. A fatwa by
the Islamic Supreme Council of America states
that a violent jihad to defend Islam should only
take place under the following circumstances:

- "There are aggressive designs against
  Islam; and
- there are concerted efforts to eject Muslims
  from their legally acquired property; and
- that military campaigns are being
  launched to eradicate them."
- The council further explains, "It cannot
  be over-emphasized that Islam upholds
  the values of reason, balance and
  responsibility in the conduct of its worldly
  affairs."[3]

*Taliban fighters prepare for action in Afghanistan in 1996.
The Taliban has been linked to al-Qaeda.*

al-Qaeda training camps in Sudan and
Afghanistan.

Al-Qaeda followed this with an attack on a US
Navy ship, the USS *Cole*, in 2000. It was in the port
of Aden, a city in Yemen on the Arabian Peninsula.
Two suicide attackers used a motorboat filled with
explosives to ram the side of the ship, killing 17
US sailors. A Yemen court would later charge six

suspected al-Qaeda members in connection with the crime. But bin Laden's largest attack was yet to happen: the September 11, 2001, attacks on US soil.

PLANNING A JIHAD

After the events of 9/11, a special commission investigated how the attacks happened. The commission determined that the attacks were in the planning stages as early as 1996, and they were the idea of Khalid Sheikh Mohammed. In late 1998 or early 1999, bin Laden gave him the go-ahead to start making preparations for the attack. Mohammad asked bin Laden for money and men. The original plan called for as many as ten airplanes and more targets, including places on the West Coast of the United States, as well as bridges and at least one nuclear reactor. According to an article in the BBC News:

USS *Cole*

The 9/11 Commission expressed the opinion that US President Bill Clinton should have ordered military retaliation after the bombing of the USS *Cole*. The lack of action gave al-Qaeda reason to continue the terrorist activities that culminated in the 9/11 attacks. "We now know from debriefings of captured al Qaeda leaders that the fact that they did the *Cole* attack and nothing happened did embolden them," former White House Director of Counter terrorism Richard Clarke said.[6]

Ayman al-Zawahiri, left, meets with bin Laden in this undated video from Arabic television station al-Jazeera.

The original plan was to pick five targets on the East Coast, and five on the West Coast, but Bin Laden did not believe that was practical, the reports state. Initially, Osama Bin Laden offered Khalid Mohammed four men—two Saudis and two Yemenis. The two Saudis—Khalid al-Mihdhar and Nawaf al-Hazmi—were on the plane that was flown into the Pentagon. But the two Yemenis—Walid Muhammed Bin Attash and Abu Bara al-Yemeni—were unable to obtain US visas, and were diverted to work on the Asian hijack plans.[5]

Bin Laden decided to use Saudi Arabian men because they could easily get visas to enter the United States. The original men were sent to Afghanistan for training in one of bin Laden's camps. They were taught fighting skills but were not really trained to fly jet planes. They also learned how to blend into US society, how to research timetables for airline flights, and how to use telephone books.

The intended hijackers arrived in the United States in 2000 and were enrolled in pilot training courses in Florida. In July 2001, the final targets for the attacks were determined, and bin Laden indicated that he wanted the plan to be carried out as quickly as possible.

Bin Laden's plans culminated in the attacks on the World Trade Center's twin towers, the Pentagon, and a thwarted attack on the White House or US Capitol. As the attacks

Asian Hijacking Plans

In 2003, US officials interrogated Khalid Sheikh Mohammed about the plans for 9/11. He told them the original plan for the terrorist attacks involved ten planes, not four. At the same time the planes were hijacked in the United States, there were supposed to be simultaneous airplane bombings or hijackings in Southeast Asia. This was a holdover from an earlier terrorist plot, the Bojinka Plot, which was planned in the mid-1990s. The Bojinka Plot would have blown up 12 airliners and approximately 4,000 passengers on flights from Asia to the United States.

unfolded with the departure of four airplane flights on that crisp September morning, bin Laden's great jihad against the United States was finally taking place.

During the terrorist attacks of September 11, 2001,
an airplane crashed into the Pentagon in Washington, DC.

On September 20, 2001, George W. Bush addressed Congress and asked the US public to prepare for a long war against terrorism.

THE UNITED STATES FIGHTS BACK

On October 7, 2001, not even a month after the terrorist attacks, bin Laden released a videotaped message:

There is America, full of fear from its north to its south, from its west to its east. Thank God for that. What America is tasting now, is something insignificant compared to what we have tasted for scores of years. Our nation (the Islamic world) has been tasting this humiliation and this degradation for more than 80 years. Its sons are killed, its blood is shed, its sanctuaries are attacked, and no one hears and no one heeds.[1]

Bin Laden also said no one in the United States would feel safe until the Islamic world felt safe from the West. That same day, US President George W. Bush responded to the 9/11 attacks and introduced Operation Enduring Freedom:

On my orders, the United States military has begun strikes against al-Qaida [sic] terrorist training camps and military installations of the Taliban regime in Afghanistan. These carefully targeted actions are designed to disrupt the use of Afghanistan as a terrorist base of operations and to attack the military capability of the Taliban regime. We're a peaceful nation. . . . Yet, as we have learned, so suddenly and so tragically, there can be no peace in a world of sudden terror. In the face of today's new threat, the only way to pursue peace is to pursue those who threaten it. We did not ask for this mission, but we will fulfill it.[2]

The US government had asked the Taliban in Afghanistan to turn over al-Qaeda and its leader.

The Taliban agreed, but only if the United States could clearly show that al-Qaeda was responsible for the 9/11 attacks. The Taliban ultimately claimed there was no hard evidence linking bin Laden to the 9/11 attacks. Operation Enduring Freedom then overthrew the Taliban regime in Afghanistan, forcing the group to flee to Pakistan.

The Battle of Tora Bora

The United States was now fighting in Afghanistan and searching for bin Laden and al-Qaeda's base. On November 12, 2001, bin Laden was in Jalalabad, outside of Kabul, giving a speech to his supporters. According to two tribal leaders who attended the speech, bin Laden proclaimed, "The Americans had a plan to invade, but if we are united and believe in Allah, we'll teach them a lesson, the same one we taught the Russians."[3]

As the bombing of Kabul became heavier, bin Laden and his supporters fled in armored vehicles and trucks. They headed for Tora Bora, a system of fortified man-made caves located in the White Mountains of eastern Afghanistan. Here bin Laden and his troops hid while the US and British Special Forces bombed the area, beginning on December 5.

It is estimated that as many as 2,000 al-Qaeda supporters were hidden inside the caves. Three dozen US Special Forces troops were located at the base of the mountain to assist the Afghan fighters who were already in place.

The US forces eventually captured Tora Bora with ground troops and air strikes, even though the heavily armed al-Qaeda fighters had the advantage of the caves and the higher elevation to help defend themselves. By December 17, the US forces were able to enter the caves. But they found that bin Laden had escaped:

Tora Bora

What were the tunnels and caves at Tora Bora really like? Mary Ann Weaver described the complex for an article in the *New York Times* in 2005:

Tora Bora was a fortress of snow-capped peaks, steep valleys and fortified caves. Its miles of tunnels, bunkers and base camps, dug deeply into the steep rock walls, had been part of a C.I.A.-financed complex built for the mujahideen. . . . The cave complex had been so refined that it was said to have its own ventilation system and a power system created by a series of hydroelectric generators; bin Laden is believed to have designed the latter. Tora Bora's walls and the floors of its hundreds of rooms were finished and smooth and extended some 350 yards into the granite mountain that enveloped them.[4]

The cave complex was located approximately 35 miles (56 km) southwest of the city of Jalalabad, 13,000 feet (3,962 m) above sea level. Some stories claim that bin Laden got heavy construction equipment from his father's company and drove the bulldozers himself in order to finish his mountain hideout.

*Coalition forces search the area of Tora Bora
for clues about the location of Taliban and al-Qaeda forces.*

On or about Dec. 16, 2001, according to American intelligence estimates, bin Laden left Tora Bora for the last time, accompanied by bodyguards and aides. Other Qaeda [sic] leaders dispersed by different routes, but bin Laden and his men are believed to have journeyed on horseback directly south toward Pakistan, crossing through . . . mountain passes and over . . . little-known smugglers' trails. And all along the route, in the dozens of villages and towns on *both sides of the frontier, the Pashtun tribes would have lighted campfires along the way to guide the horsemen.*[5]

Bin Laden had escaped just when the US forces had him in their sights. According to bin Laden's account of the Battle of Tora Bora:

A severe and fierce bombardment began . . . not one second passed without warplanes hovering over our heads . . . [America] exhausted all efforts to blow up and annihilate this tiny spot—wiping it out altogether. . . . Despite all this, we blocked their daily attacks, sending them back defeated, bearing their dead and wounded. . . . And not once did American forces dare storm our positions! What clearer proof of their cowardice, fear, and lies concerning the myth of their alleged power is out there?![6]

Al-Qaeda and the Taliban regrouped, setting up new headquarters in Pakistan. Some experts assert that they were able

The Golden Chain

In March 2002, Bosnian police raided the Benevolence International Foundation in Sarajevo. They found thousands of pages of documents related to al-Qaeda, including letters, meeting notes, and photos. The CIA gained possession of the materials, which they refer to as the "Golden Chain." Among the documents was a list that is believed to contain the names of people who sponsored al-Qaeda. The list includes at least 20 financial sponsors from Saudi Arabia and the Persian Gulf states, including bankers, businessmen, and former ministers.

to regroup because the United States turned its attention to a war in Iraq. In the next year, al-Qaeda would go on to plan or sponsor more terrorist attacks around the world.

FRESH ATTACKS

In October 2002, more than 200 people were killed when a suicide bomber blew up a crowded nightclub in Bali. A month later, an audiotape of bin Laden surfaced. He claimed responsibility for the Bali attack, as well as others, and threatened any nation that supported the United States after the 9/11 attacks.

Another attack took place in Madrid, Spain, in March 2004. Terrorists used cell phones to detonate ten bombs on Madrid's commuter trains. A total of 190 people died, and hundreds more were wounded. Al-Qaeda supposedly had no direct connection to the incident, but the terrorists were allegedly inspired by bin Laden's group and their tactics.

In July 2005, another attack took place in London, England. Four suicide bombers detonated bombs on three London trains and one bus during the morning rush hour. Fifty-two people died and more than 700 were injured. The city's transportation system was crippled for days. Later, these bombings were linked directly to al-Qaeda.

"WE WILL FIND YOU"

The United States had failed to capture bin Laden. His terrorist attacks continued, including a foiled attempt to blow up passenger planes headed for the United States in December 2001. The United States was not willing to give up the search. On the fifth anniversary of 9/11, President George W. Bush addressed the nation:

> Osama Bin Laden and other terrorists are still in hiding. Our message to them is clear: No matter how long it takes, America will find you, and we will bring you to justice. . . . Five years after Nine-Eleven, our enemies have not succeeded in launching another attack on our soil—

Guantanamo Bay

Guantanamo Bay is a US detention camp on the island of Cuba. Many prisoners from Iraq and Afghanistan, including those with alleged ties to al-Qaeda, were taken there. After prisoners complained of conditions and treatment there, the United Nations Commission on Human Rights investigated. The organization found there had been incidents of torture, mistreatment, and abuse at the camp. According to the UN report, prisoners on hunger strikes had been force-fed through nasal tubes. Others were interrogated in conditions that included solitary confinement and exposure to extreme heat, cold, noise, or light. The United Nations recommended closing the base. As of 2011 it was still open, although many prisoners had been transferred to other facilities.

but they have not been idle. Al Qaeda and those inspired by its hateful ideology have carried out terrorist attacks in more than two dozen nations.[7]

The hunt for Osama bin Laden was far from over.

This double-decker bus in Tavistock Square, London,
was one target of the July 2005 terrorist attack.

*US Marines in Afghanistan work with local civilians
as part of Operation Enduring Freedom.*

The Hunt Is On

*I*t seemed the United States had lost track
of bin Laden. The CIA's special unit,
which had sought bin Laden and al-Qaeda even
before 9/11, was disbanded in 2006. The CIA
claimed that the terrorist attacks inspired by

al-Qaeda were now being carried out independently without bin Laden and his top deputies. An Associated Press report stated, "The CIA said hunting bin Laden remains a priority, but resources needed to be directed toward other people and groups likely to initiate new attacks."[1]

THE WAR ON TERROR

Meanwhile, the United States and other allies around the world continued to wage a war against terrorists. President Bush referred to this as the War on Terror, and it was a term applied to many campaigns against terrorists, including Operation Enduring Freedom in Afghanistan and military actions in the Philippines and Somalia. Many of these operations were efforts to keep radical Islamic governments from gaining footholds. The United States was also involved in the Iraq war. Iraq had been a known sponsor of terrorism. It had also been known to use chemical weapons against Iranians and Kurds. Its terrorism, however, was based on secular politics, not religion.

Even though someone claiming to be bin Laden was broadcasting messages from time to time, the CIA said it had no idea where he was. There were

Wikileaks

The Web site *Wikileaks* publishes "leaked" documents from governments, religious organizations, corporations, and other organizations. These documents are usually about some sort of misconduct or were formerly classified, and the site exposes these documents to the public. It tries to keep its contributors anonymous. Publicizing these types of documents is illegal, and the founder of the Web site was arrested and jailed in Sweden and faces charges in other countries as well.

many rumors of secret hideouts and activities supposedly masterminded by bin Laden, but the CIA said it had no real intelligence as to his whereabouts. This, however, would later be disputed by reports uncovered by Wikileaks, a Web site dedicated to revealing secret information, which said that bin Laden had been seen regularly at meetings in small villages on the Afghanistan-Pakistan border.

In December 2005, there was another tantalizing clue about bin Laden's whereabouts. Atiyah, a senior al-Qaeda official and a supposed member of bin Laden's high command, wrote a letter to Abu Musab al-Zarqawi, the leader of al-Qaeda in Iraq. In it, Atiyah claimed to be writing from a new hideout in Waziristan, Pakistan. According to the *Washington Post*:

> *"I am with them," Atiyah writes Zarqawi of the high command, "and they have some comments about some of*

A letter sent to Abu Musab al-Zarqawi proved bin Laden was still alive.

your circumstances." The "brothers," he writes, "wish that they had a way to talk to you and advise you, and to guide and instruct you; however, they too are occupied with vicious *enemies here." . . . Atiyah orders him not to make "any decision on a comprehensive issue" without consulting bin Laden, Zawahiri and the other "brothers."*[2]

The letter seemed to prove that bin Laden was still alive, despite rumors that he had been killed in the Tora Bora battle or had died of disease. It even suggested that the leadership of al-Qaeda was going through difficulties. It also gave US officials an idea of where he might be.

RETURN TO TORA BORA

The United States continued to search for bin Laden and his followers, as well as Taliban strongholds and leaders. Operation Redwing in 2005 failed to take out a Taliban cell, and US Navy SEALs and other Special Forces soldiers were killed.

On June 7, 2006, Abu Musab al-Zarqawi was killed in an air strike in Iraq. His death prompted another message from bin Laden. The message eulogizing al-Zarqawi proved that bin Laden was not only alive, but also able to send out messages quickly in response to recent events. Bin Laden addressed his message to President Bush, according to a Cable News Network (CNN) article:

*I say to Bush, you should deliver the body (of al-Zarqawi)
to his family, and don't be too happy. Our flag hasn't fallen,
thanks be to God. It has passed from one lion to another lion
in Islam. . . . We will continue, God willing, to fight you and
your allies everywhere, in Iraq, Afghanistan, Somalia and
Sudan, until we drain your money and kill your men and send
you home defeated,
God willing, as we
defeated you before,
thanks to God, in
Somalia.[3]*

In July, what
was believed to
be bin Laden's
voice was heard
again. He issued
a statement
saying Somalis
should fight to
establish an Islamic
government.
He added that
al-Qaeda would
fight against any

Operation Redwing

Operation Redwing took place on June 28,
2005. It involved four members of a US Navy
SEAL team. Their mission was to kill or capture Ahmad Shah, also known as Commander
Ismail, a Taliban leader rumored to be in
Asadabad, Afghanistan. The SEAL team made
it into the area, but a group of local farmers
stumbled upon their hiding place. The SEALs
let the herders go. A short time later, a group of
Afghan fighters attacked the SEALs.

Fighting lasted almost an hour, and three
members of the SEAL team were killed. The
fourth, Marcus Luttrell, was wounded. He was
discovered and protected by local villagers,
who sent a message to the nearest military
camp and got help for Luttrell. A rescue helicopter with 16 military personnel was shot
down with a rocket grenade. Ahmad Shah later
boasted that he had set a trap for the US forces:
"We certainly know that when the American
army comes under pressure and they get hit,
they will try to help their friends. It is the law of
the battlefield."[4]

Western government that attempted to interfere. But the message did not lead US forces to his hiding place.

By 2006, many US officials assumed bin Laden was hiding in Pakistan. It was a country where he was popular and had supporters, and it was a place he knew well. US intelligence officials admitted that they would have to be "extraordinarily lucky" to find and capture him there.[5]

In September 2006, Pakistani president Pervez Musharraf announced for the first time that bin Laden might be hiding in his country. Previously, the Pakistani government had claimed the al-Qaeda leader's location was a mystery. But at a meeting in New York City, President Musharraf admitted that his government might know the general whereabouts of bin Laden.

In 2007, US forces returned to the caves and tunnels of Tora Bora, using air attacks on the complex where al-Qaeda and Taliban forces

Eyes in the Sky

The Predator and the Reaper are unmanned aircraft. The Predator is intended to fly long distances at low altitudes in order to perform surveillance and reconnaissance missions. It has radar as well as video and infrared cameras, and it uses a satellite link to send images to military forces on the ground. There is also a version that can be armed with a missile. The Reaper is an expanded version of the Predator, with a secure voice relay, a more powerful engine, wing deicing systems for colder climates, and the ability to survey a wider area.

A Predator unmanned aircraft prepares for take-off.

were still known to be planning and training for attacks on both Afghanistan and Pakistan. There had been a small chance that bin Laden himself would be there. But the military action failed to catch its number-one target.

As Bush approached the end of his presidency in 2008, he seemed more determined than ever to bring Osama bin Laden to justice. In June 2008, US and British Special Forces conducted a mission to find bin Laden in Pakistan. The mission used

Predator and Reaper unmanned aerial vehicles that could fly over suspected terrorist strongholds and drop missiles. President Bush wanted to apprehend bin Laden before he left office. But the efforts did not succeed, and President Bush's administration ended with the inauguration of President Barack Obama in January 2009.

A DEAD END?

In a 2009 interview with George Stephanopoulos on ABC's *Good Morning America* television show, Defense Secretary Robert Gates claimed that the US government had no idea where bin Laden was:

GATES. Well, we don't know for a fact where Osama bin Laden is. If we did, we'd go get him.

STEPHANOPOULOS. What was the last time we had any good intelligence on where he was?

GATES. I think it's been years.

STEPHANOPOULOS. Years?!

GATES. I think so.[6]

It seemed that Osama bin Laden had eluded the United States. Would he ever be stopped?

Robert Gates speaks to the troops. Gates admitted the Obama administration
had little information about bin Laden's whereabouts in 2009.

*When Barack Obama became president,
he remained committed to finding bin Laden.*

"WE WILL KILL
BIN LADEN"

uring a debate in October 2008, before
he won the presidential election, Barack
Obama stated clearly, "We will kill bin Laden. We
will crush al Qaeda. That has to be our biggest
national security priority."[1] He was responding to

what had been seen as the Bush administration's reluctance to pursue bin Laden when there seemed to be no solid clues about his whereabouts. The US government was offering a $25 million reward for information that led to the capture of bin Laden, but people familiar with the region where he might be hiding said that those who lived there would consider it dishonorable to take the money and turn in bin Laden.

By January 2009, President Obama was no longer saying that bin Laden necessarily had to be killed. "My preference obviously would be to capture or kill him. . . . But if we have so tightened the noose that he's in a cave somewhere and can't even communicate . . . then we will meet our goal of protecting America."[2]

At that same time, another audiotape believed to feature bin Laden surfaced. In it, bin Laden taunted President Bush and claimed that President Obama would have to choose between military defeat and economic crisis.

More Rumors

Despite the political changeover from Bush to Obama, the US military was still trying to pinpoint bin Laden's location. In March 2009, it was suggested that he might be hiding out in the Chitral region of northern Pakistan, an area of tall peaks and deep valleys in the Hindu Kush Mountains that was difficult to reach. US spy planes had begun to make regular reconnaissance flights there. It was also rumored that captured al-Qaeda members had confirmed that bin Laden was hiding in Chitral. However, Pakistani leaders claimed there was no evidence that bin Laden was even alive. Other sources claimed he was still in Afghanistan, including Nasser al-Bahria, former bodyguard of bin Laden. Al-Bahria explained that the tribes that live along the Afghanistan and Pakistan border would protect bin Laden, explaining,

> These tribes, bin Laden has known them for the last 20 years. He help them financially and materially in the '80s and these tribes also, I think it's an important factor, are more loyal to the religion than to the typical tribal character, which mean [sic] that it's not very easy to bribe them. [3]

By October 2010, North Atlantic Treaty Organization (NATO) officials claimed to have more information about bin Laden's whereabouts. They asserted that he was not holed up in a cave or living

*If members of the close-knit tribes of Pakistan and Afghanistan were
hiding bin Laden, they would be unlikely to turn him in.*

in a remote wilderness. The difficulty was that he was
most likely on the move. Explained one official, "If
we knew where he was—in a house, an apartment, a
villa or an underground cave or bunker—we would
have gotten him. . . . We can't rule out he may be in
a cave one day and a house in a city on another."[4]

Locating al-Qaeda couriers was a priority for the
CIA in their hunt for bin Laden. In 1998, the US
military had bombed his hideouts in Afghanistan
and Sudan simply by tracing a satellite phone call

made by one of his men. Therefore, bin Laden would no longer use phones to communicate and could not be traced that way anymore. It was the identification of one of the al-Qaeda couriers that ultimately led the CIA to bin Laden's location.

A Covert Operation

By late 2010, the Obama administration felt that it had enough information about bin Laden's whereabouts to begin a covert operation to capture him. According to a CNN article:

> Four years ago, US officials [uncovered] the identity of a trusted bin Laden courier—later identified as a Kuwaiti named Abu Ahmad—whom they believed may have been living with and protecting the al Qaeda leader. Two years later, investigators [identified] parts of Pakistan where the courier and his brother lived.[5]

Money

The surveillance effort to locate bin Laden was so expensive that the CIA had to go before the US Congress in December 2010 in order to get permission to redistribute tens of millions of dollars from other budgets in order to pay for it.

After a series of wiretaps and the surveillance of a man believed to be one of bin Laden's couriers, the CIA was able to trace bin Laden to a compound located in Bilal Town, Abbottabad, Pakistan, approximately 100 miles (160 km) from the Afghan border. The location and construction of the compound made it clear that someone of importance was hiding there. The CIA rented a safe house in Abbottabad, and together with other intelligence agencies, began collecting information about the compound and bin Laden's possible presence there.

"Dark Arts and Domesticity"

Videos seized after the raid on bin Laden's compound painted a picture of his life there, according to a *New York Times* article:

The world's most wanted terrorist lived his last five years imprisoned behind the barbed wire and high walls of his home in Abbottabad, Pakistan, his days consumed by dark arts and domesticity. . . . While his physical world had shrunk to two indoor rooms and daily pacing in his courtyard, Bin Laden was still revered at home—by his three wives, by his children and by the tight, interconnected circle of loyalists in the compound.[6]

At home in the compound, bin Laden relied on a computer to connect himself to the outside world and run his terror network. He used couriers to send flash drives to followers and to receive information from them in return. Other videos recovered from the compound show bin Laden watching himself on television and practicing lines in front of a mirror. He dyed his beard black to make his recordings. From this information, officials conclude that bin Laden was concerned about his image.

Neptune Spear

The code name for the operation that captured bin Laden took its name from classical mythology. Neptune was the ancient Roman god of the sea. Neptune's spear, a trident, appears on the logo of the SEALs.

Once enough intelligence had been gathered to verify bin Laden's whereabouts, President Obama authorized a covert operation on April 29, 2011, code-named Operation Neptune Spear. It would be a CIA operation, but carried out by US Navy SEALs from the US Naval Special Warfare Development Group. The CIA's role in Operation Neptune Spear was over before the actual raid took place. A US official explained, "The CIA's job was to find and fix," or identify and locate an important target. "The intelligence work was as complete as it was going to be, and it was the military's turn to finish the target."[7] The raid on bin Laden's compound would be launched from Afghanistan, with the help of CIA operatives in the area. On Sunday, May 1, Operation Neptune Spear went into action.

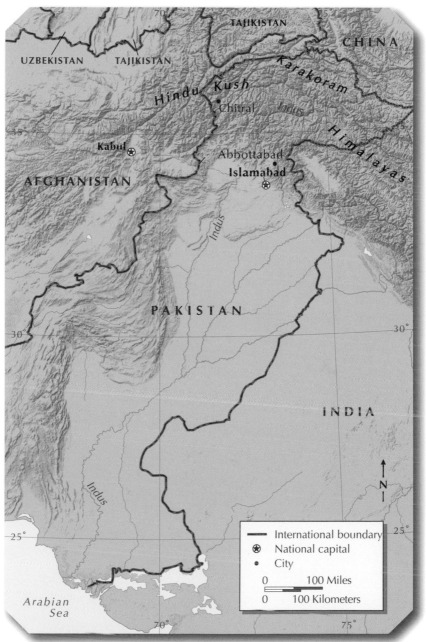

*Bin Laden was believed to be hiding somewhere in Afghanistan
or Pakistan; he was found in Abbottabad, Pakistan.*

President Obama and members of his administration watch the satellite images of Operation Neptune Spear.

"We Got Him"

On Sunday, May 1, 2011, President Obama joined his staff in the White House Situation Room. There, through satellite feeds, they would watch the progress of Operation Neptune Spear. Over the next hour, they watched as the satellite link faded in and out. "The minutes passed like days," one of the officials recalled.[1]

Inside the Compound

Bin Laden's compound was located in an upscale neighborhood with nice houses, open fields, and a nearby golf course. It was only minutes away from a Pakistani military academy. However, the compound was clearly not just another luxury home, as it was walled and fenced. As a US intelligence operative said:

> Once we came across this compound, we paid close attention to it because it became clear that whoever was living here was trying to maintain a very discreet profile. It had the appearance of a fortress.[2]

The compound was triangular in shape, enclosing a three-story house as well as other buildings. A ten-foot- (3-m-) high wall, topped with barbed

Living the Good Life

President Obama's chief counterterrorism adviser commented on the fact that bin Laden was located in such luxurious surroundings, far from any al-Qaeda action. "Here is bin Laden, who has been calling for these attacks, living in this million-dollar-plus compound, living in an area that is far removed from the front. I think this really speaks to just how false his narrative has been over the years."[3]

wire, surrounded it. Inside, another seven-foot- (2-m-) high privacy fence surrounded bin Laden's actual residence, screening his upper level balcony from sight. The walls were higher and thicker than a regular residence. A long, walled driveway with gates at both ends had been designed to trap intruders.

US intelligence had used a spy satellite to watch the compound for many months preceding the attack until they were confident they had found bin Laden's hideout.

By the time of the raid, the SEAL team involved in the raid, Navy SEAL Team Six, also knew the compound well. They had been training in a replica of it.

THE RAID

Just before 1 a.m. local time, early Monday morning in Pakistan, two helicopters with 24 Navy SEALs on board swooped into the compound.

Code Name Geronimo

SEAL Team Six had two code words ready in advance: *Jackpot* was the code name for bin Laden himself, and *Geronimo* was the code name for the overall operation. The original Geronimo was an Apache leader who fought against the US and Mexico expansion into native Apache lands and managed to evade capture for many years. The choice of this code name has angered many Native Americans, who see it as connecting them with terrorism.

Bin Laden's compound in Abbottabad

It was just before 5 p.m. Sunday in Washington DC. One helicopter landed to let the soldiers out. Other soldiers used ropes to descend from the second helicopter, which lost altitude and was damaged when it landed hard beside one of the compound's walls. They would only be on the ground for approximately 40 minutes.

Most of the SEALs were immediately engaged in fighting with bin Laden's men as they made their way past several small buildings to the actual residence. Finally reaching the house, the SEALs searched for bin Laden, according to an article in *Newsweek*:

A Stealth Helicopter?

Some sources speculate that the helicopter that crashed in bin Laden's compound was actually a new secret stealth helicopter, never before actually seen. These sources believe it was a modified Black Hawk helicopter, with reduced rotor noise and other elements that would make it harder to detect. After the raid, the United States asked Pakistan to return the remnants of the helicopter, but the Pakistanis allegedly commented that the Chinese government was also very interested in looking at the wreckage. Pakistan returned the helicopter pieces to the US military three weeks after the raid.

> *As [the SEALS] climbed to the top floor, bin Laden's son came onto the stairs, brandishing a weapon. They took him down. As they entered the bedroom, bin Laden's wife rushed at them. She was shot in the leg. And then there was the man himself, unarmed. . . . Bin Laden took a bullet to the chest. Then another to the head. "Geronimo EKIA," came the report heard at Langley and the White House. Enemy killed in action.[4]*

It was 1:15 a.m. local time on Monday, May 2. Osama bin Laden was dead. No members of SEAL Team Six were injured. The hunt for bin Laden was finally over. In the Situation Room at the White House, President Obama said, "We got him."[5]

GETTING OUT

The SEAL team quickly swept through the compound, collecting documents and computers that would hopefully provide valuable information for US intelligence about al-Qaeda. Meanwhile, one of bin Laden's wives confirmed his identity, and a photograph of the dead man's face was relayed to the United States. There, experts would run the image through a facial recognition software program. The women and children still in the compound

Three Down . . .

In just a little over a month's time during the spring of 2011, three senior al-Qaeda leaders were killed around the world. In addition to Osama bin Laden's death, Ilyas Kashmiri, a top al-Qaeda militant, was killed in Pakistan on June 3. He was believed to be responsible for planning the 2008 massacre in Mumbai, as well as an attempted attack on the US company Lockheed-Martin, which manufactures drone planes for the US military. Ironically, Kashmiri himself was killed by a drone plane. Then on June 11, Somalia military forces announced that they had killed Fazul Abdullah Mohammed, who had planned the 1998 embassy bombings in Kenya and Tanzania. He was killed at a checkpoint in Somalia. Forces there did not even realize they had killed an al-Qaeda leader until later because Fazul was traveling under a false passport. Secretary of State Hillary Clinton spoke about Mohammed's death, calling it:

a significant blow to Al Qaeda, its extremist allies, and its operations in East Africa. It is a just end for a terrorist who brought so much death and pain to so many innocents in Nairobi and Dar es Salaam and elsewhere—Tanzanians, Kenyans, Somalis, and our own embassy personnel.[6]

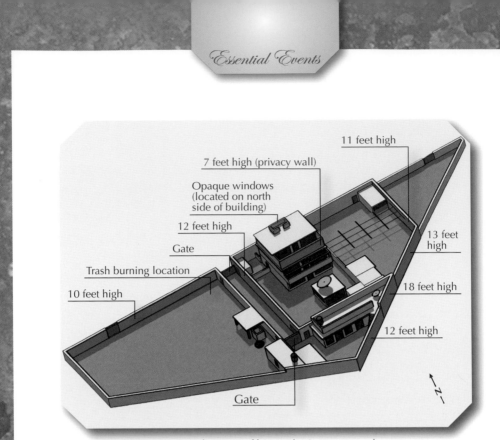

A CIA diagram of bin Laden's compound

were moved to safety, and the damaged SEAL helicopter was destroyed. As the SEALs loaded the body onto the remaining helicopter, the results of the recognition software were delivered: it was bin Laden. This would later be further confirmed by a DNA comparison with a member of bin Laden's family.

The SEALs had successfully eluded Pakistani radar when they flew in, but they knew that any moment Pakistani jets might arrive and engage in firing on them. The US had not asked Pakistan for permission to invade its territory, and the SEALs knew the Pakistan military might retaliate. However, the SEALs left the area without further combat.

The helicopters made their way first to Bagram Air Base in Afghanistan for further identification of bin Laden's corpse. Then the body was taken to the USS *Carl Vinson*, a US aircraft carrier located in the Arabian Sea.

The US government knew that it was risky for bin Laden to have an actual grave, since it would likely become a shrine for other terrorists. According to Islamic custom, bodies are usually buried in the ground quickly, without a coffin, within 24 hours. Government sources confirm bin Laden's burial was conducted according to Islamic law. An officer read religious remarks that were translated by a native Arabic speaker.

A Sister's DNA

Approximately one year before bin Laden's death, his sister died of brain cancer in a hospital in Boston, Massachusetts. After her death, samples of her tissue were collected by the government, most likely to use her DNA for positive identification in the event of bin Laden's death. After his death in the Pakistan raid, the DNA from his sister, according to the government, proved that the body was indeed bin Laden, with a 99.9 percent probability.

The speaker's identity was not released and it is not know if the speaker was an Islamic clergy member. According to a *Time* magazine article:

> *There, his body was washed and wrapped in a white sheet, then dropped overboard. There would be no grave for his admirers to venerate. The face that haunted the Western world, the eyes that looked on the blazing towers with pride of authorship, sank sightless beneath the waves.* [7]

Bin Laden's body was buried at sea from the USS Carl Vinson.

*New Yorkers celebrated the death of Osama bin Laden
near Ground Zero on May 2, 2011.*

The World Reacts

At 11:35 p.m. eastern standard time on May 1, President Obama called a press conference. Speaking on live television from the White House, he announced Osama bin Laden's death, adding:

Today, at my direction, the United States launched a targeted operation against that compound in Abbottabad, Pakistan. A small team of Americans carried out the operation with extraordinary courage and capability. No Americans were harmed. They took care to avoid civilian casualties. After a firefight, they killed Osama bin Laden and took custody of his body. . . . The death of bin Laden marks the most significant achievement to date in our nation's effort to defeat al Qaeda.[1]

CELEBRATING IN THE STREETS

Almost as soon as President Obama's speech was finished, people began gathering in public places all over the United States to celebrate the death of the terrorist. In particular, they gathered at Ground Zero in New York City, the site of the terrible 9/11 attacks not quite ten years before. According to *Time* magazine:

"Earlier this evening, President Obama called to inform me that American forces killed Osama bin Laden. . . . I congratulated him and the men and women of our military and intelligence communities who devoted their lives to this mission. They have our everlasting gratitude. This momentous achievement marks a victory for America, for people who seek peace around the world, and for all those who lost loved ones on September 11, 2001. The fight against terror goes on, but tonight America has sent an unmistakable message: No matter how long it takes, justice will be done."[2]

—*Former president George W. Bush reacting to the news of bin Laden's death*

"I Will Always Remember"

Ben Hughes, a college student in Georgia, was only in sixth grade when the 9/11 attacks occurred, but he remembered it as the first time in his life that he felt helpless. When he heard the news of bin Laden's death, he posted a message on Facebook: "In the years since [9/11] I have marked every year with a solid time of reflection and silence. And I will always remember also that I was on a flight between Charlotte, NC, and Savannah, GA, when the pilot came over the loudspeaker to announce that Osama bin Laden had been killed."[5]

There was perhaps no place more fitting to go than the place where it all began. As President Obama wrapped up his remarks . . . a few people started to gather at New York City's Ground Zero. They kept coming. By the time a man shinnied up a lamppost around midnight and sprayed bottles of champagne over the crowd, several hundred people had gathered. . . . This colorful crowd, American flags draped around their necks, sang the national anthem, "God Bless the U.S.A." and "America, the Beautiful" in spurts of unison. They chanted "U.S.A.! U.S.A.! U.S.A.!"[3]

Others came to pay tribute to the victims of 9/11, including many who had lost friends or relatives. As one woman who had lost a family friend on 9/11 said, "This is a little bit of closure. We finally have some peace in our lives."[4]

Others gathered at Times Square, the Pentagon, and the

White House. At a major league baseball game in Philadelphia, fans began chanting "USA!" when they heard the news. Students at colleges and universities all over the country had spontaneous celebrations, including fireworks, chanting, and flag-waving.

A Sense of Caution

Not everyone was celebrating unconditionally. In the Middle East, particularly in Iraq and among members of the Taliban, the news of bin Laden's death brought criticism and even some threats of reprisals. In Pakistan, people carried pictures of bin Laden and shouted anti-American slogans. Several Middle Eastern countries announced that the death of bin Laden meant the United States no longer had an excuse to occupy their territories. Others encouraged Muslim jihadists to retaliate against Americans. Diplomatic alerts warned US embassies and citizens around the world to prepare for attacks.

Even countries that supported the US actions were cautious. According to Ken Livingstone, a British politician:

*Pakistani demonstrators protested the death
of Osama bin Laden in Quetta, Pakistan.*

I just looked at [the pictures of Americans celebrating Bin
Laden's death] and realised that it would increase the likelihood
of a terror attack on London. . . . We should have captured

*[bin Laden] and put him on trial. It's a simple point—are we
gangsters or a Western democracy based on the rule of law?
This undermines any commitment to democracy and trial by
jury and makes Obama look like some sort of mobster.*[6]

In addition, some legal experts argued that
the killing of bin Laden was illegal according
to international law. These experts questioned
whether the SEALs's shooting of bin Laden could
be considered self-defense, since bin Laden was
unarmed when he was killed. If the shooting was not
self-defense, these experts argued that bin Laden
should have been arrested to face a trial. In addition,
legal experts worried the United States violated
Pakistan's sovereignty, or right to govern itself, by
carrying out the mission without Pakistan's consent.
In contrast, the US government argues its actions
were legal. Its position is that international law allows
it to defend itself against the leaders of terrorist
organizations that carry out attacks on US soil. In
addition, the government believes the Navy SEALs
acted within the law by killing bin Laden without
attempting to arrest him. The SEALs had the right to
assume bin Laden was likely lethally armed and shoot
him on sight.

PAKISTAN'S ROLE

The raid on bin Laden's compound and his resulting death also created strain between the United States and Pakistan. Pakistan expressed displeasure at US forces carrying out a mission within their country without their knowledge. Americans themselves now wondered if Pakistan had known about bin Laden's presence all along and kept it a secret, and if the country could be trusted in the future. In planning the May 2 raid, President Obama had been presented with an option for conducting a joint raid with Pakistan on bin Laden's compound. He had rejected the plan, fearing the information would be leaked by Pakistan to bin Laden before the raid could take place.

Some Pakistanis also feared retaliation against their country for the terrorist's death. Tasneen Nooran, a former Pakistani secretary

Wives' Tales

After his death, the United States was able to speak to three of bin Laden's wives. One claimed he had lived in Pakistan for seven years. Another claimed he had moved there in 2006. The women, from Yemen and Saudi Arabia, were taken into custody after the raid on bin Laden's compound and were still being held in the summer of 2011, although there were plans to return them to their home countries.

for the Interior, said, "The extremist group in Pakistan will hold the government responsible . . . and will hold the state responsible. I think you will see more terrorism here in retaliation."[7]

Regardless of the role Pakistan did or did not play in the raid or in aiding bin Laden, the relationship between Pakistan and the United States was strained as a result of bin Laden's death. It is important for the United States to maintain a working relationship with Pakistan because terrorists thrive in the country's tribal regions and could seize Pakistan's atomic weapons.

Since 9/11, the United States has been at war in Afghanistan. The goals of the war are to end the Taliban insurgency and root out terrorist cells. In order to succeed in Afghanistan, the United States needs to shut down terrorist safe havens in Pakistan. The country also has several supply routes that are vital for US troops in Afghanistan. Continued violence in Afghanistan could also destabilize Pakistan.

However, partially as a result of the increased tension since bin Laden's death, the United States decreased military aid to Pakistan in July 2011.

Photos . . . or Not

In the days following the raid, there was continuing speculation as to whether or not President Obama would allow the photographs of bin Laden's dead body to be released to the public. Many people felt the photos would prove that bin Laden was actually dead and stop some of the conspiracy theory rumors. However, others felt that photos themselves—since photographs are easily altered or faked today—would never be conclusive proof. It was said that the photographs were

Conspiracy Theories

Almost as soon as bin Laden's death was announced to the world, conspiracy theories surfaced. Conspiracy theories are often put forward as a way to cast doubt on politicians and their motives, or to suggest that a government is not being truthful. Theories claimed that bin Laden was not actually dead, or that he had actually died many years before. Because of his burial at sea, conspiracy theorists took this as proof that bin Laden had not actually been killed. Others believed that the US government's refusal to release photos of the dead body was also proof that the famous terrorist was not dead. Some felt bin Laden's death was announced in order to improve President Obama's chances for reelection.

The US government chose not to release images of bin Laden's body. President Obama explained that he did not want graphic images to incite violence among bin Laden's followers. He further explained that releasing photos was not likely to convince conspiracy theorists: "There is no doubt that Osama bin Laden is dead. . . . Certainly there is no doubt among al-Qaeda members that he is dead. So we don't think that a photograph in and of itself is going to make any difference."[8]

also grisly. Ultimately President Obama decided not to release the photos.

Going Forward

The death of Osama bin Laden has raised the question about the future of terrorism. His death, as well as the deaths of two other top al-Qaeda figures in early 2011, has left many people speculating about the future of the terrorist group. Many feel it is the end of al-Qaeda as a global threat. As foreign policy expert Fareed Zakaria writes in a *Time* magazine article:

> *Al-Qaeda was personified by bin Laden, a man who for his followers represented courage and conviction. . . . With bin Laden's death, the cause and the man have both been extinguished. We will battle terrorists for years to come, but that does not make them a mortal threat to the Western world or its way of life. The existential danger is over.* [9]

However, six weeks after bin Laden's death, al-Qaeda had a new leader. He was Ayman al-Zawahiri, the same man whose Egyptian Islamic Jihad had merged with al-Qaeda, and who coauthored the 1998 fatwa against the United States. Al-Zawahiri has vowed to continue the jihad against the West, saying:

The man who terrified America in his life will continue to terrify it after his death. You will continue to be troubled by his famous vow: You shall not dream of security until we enjoy it and until you depart the Muslims' lands. The senior al-Qaeda leader vowed to make sacrifices needed to "deprive America of security. We will pursue the jihad until we expel the invaders from Muslim lands."[10]

It is clear from al-Zawahiri's statement that bin Laden's death has not eliminated the threat of al-Qaeda and future acts of terrorism. There will always be terrorism in some form, but perhaps the death of bin Laden will continue to diminish the power of al-Qaeda. Bin Laden's death marked a huge step in terms of controlling terrorism instead of letting terrorism control the world. ⌐

SPECIAL ISSUE   MAY 20, 2011

TIME

The cover of Time magazine broadcast bin Laden's death.
Bin Laden is dead, but the world still faces terrorist acts.

TIMELINE

1957	ca. 1974	1979
Osama bin Laden is born in Riyadh, Saudi Arabia, on March 10.	Bin Laden marries his first wife.	Bin Laden graduates from college and moves to Pakistan to join a holy war against the Soviet Union.

1989	1990	1991
The Soviet Union withdraws from Afghanistan.	The United States launches attacks on Iraq from Saudi Arabia.	Bin Laden is expelled from Saudi Arabia.

1980–1989	**1989**	**1989**
Bin Laden fights in Pakistan and Afghanistan.	Bin Laden forms al-Qaeda with Abdullah Azzam.	Azzam dies and bin Laden takes sole control of al-Qaeda.

1993	**1994**	**1996**
A bomb explodes at the World Trade Center in New York City on February 26. Bin Laden is named a coconspirator.	Saudi Arabia strips bin Laden of his citizenship. His family also disowns him.	Sudan expels bin Laden. He moves to Afghanistan.

TIMELINE

1996	1998	1998
Bin Laden declares a holy war against the United States on August 23.	Truck bombs kill 200 people in Kenya and Tanzania on August 7 and al-Qaeda takes responsibility.	Al-Qaeda merges with the Egyptian Islamic Jihad, led by Ayman al-Zawahiri.

2001	2009	2010
On December 5, US and British forces attack the Tora Bora caves near the Pakistani border where bin Laden is rumored to be hiding.	US officials claim in December that there has been no credible intelligence about bin Laden's whereabouts in years.	President Barack Obama receives intelligence that bin Laden is hiding in Abbottabad, Pakistan.

1999

Bin Laden is placed on the FBI's Most Wanted Terrorists list.

2000

Bin Laden is linked to the October 12 attack on the USS Cole.

2001

Al-Qaeda hijackers crash airplanes into the World Trade Center's two towers, the Pentagon, and a field in Pennsylvania on September 11.

2011

President Obama approves the mission Operation Neptune Spear on April 29.

2011

On May 2, Osama bin Laden is killed in a raid on his compound in Abbottabad and is later buried at sea.

2011

In June, al-Zawahiri becomes the new leader of al-Qaeda.

Essential Facts

Date of Event

May 2, 2011

Place of Event

Osama bin Laden's compound in Abbottabad, Pakistan

Key Players

- ❖ Osama bin Laden
- ❖ Members of al-Qaeda
- ❖ US Navy SEAL Team Six
- ❖ President Barack Obama
- ❖ US intelligence operatives

Highlights of Event

❖ After bin Laden and al-Qaeda claim responsibility for the 9/11 attacks, bin Laden becomes the United States' most wanted terrorist.

❖ After a battle at Tora Bora in Afghanistan in 2001, the United States loses track of bin Laden until intelligence locates him in Abbottabad, Pakistan, in 2010.

❖ On May 2, 2011, the elite Navy SEAL Team Six carries out Operation Neptune Spear by raiding bin Laden's compound and killing bin Laden. His body is then buried at sea.

Quote

"Tonight, I can report to the American people and to the world that the United States has conducted an operation that killed Osama bin Laden, the leader of Al Qaeda, and a terrorist who's responsible for the murder of thousands of innocent men, women, and children."—*President Barack Obama, May 2, 2011*

GLOSSARY

assassinate
To murder a prominent person suddenly or unexpectedly, usually for political reasons.

bombardment
An attack with bombs or artillery fire.

casualties
People who are injured or killed in an accident, event, or military operation.

cell
A small group acting as a unit within a larger organization.

disown
To refuse to acknowledge someone as belonging or being related.

dissident
A person whose attitude disagrees with established authority or doctrine.

drone
A vehicle with no driver inside that is piloted from afar.

embassy
The home and office of a diplomat who lives in a foreign country.

ethnic
Of or having to do with a group of people who have the same race, nationality, or culture.

eulogize
To praise or speak highly of.

fatwa
A religious legal pronouncement on a specific subject, often a declaration of war.

jihad
A holy war undertaken as a sacred duty by Muslims.

militia
> A group of citizens who are enrolled in the military but serve only during emergencies.

Muslim
> A person who practices the religion of Islam.

nationalism
> Devotion and loyalty to one's country.

radical
> To be in favor of extreme or drastic political reforms.

sect
> A group of people who follow a particular religious or political belief, which may be different from the accepted practice.

secular
> Having to do with worldly things, not religion or spirituality.

supremacist
> A person who believes his or her own group, especially racial or ethnic group, is superior to others.

ADDITIONAL RESOURCES

SELECTED BIBLIOGRAPHY

Fury, Dalton. *Kill Bin Laden: A Delta Force Commander's Account of the Hunt for the World's Most Wanted Man*. New York: St Martin's, 2008. Print.

"Mission Accomplished: But Are We Any Safer?" *Newsweek*, May 16, 2011. Print.

Scheuer, Michael. *Osama bin Laden*. New York: Oxford, 2011. Print.

"Special Report: The End of Bin Laden," *Time* magazine, May 20, 2011. Print.

FURTHER READINGS

Frank, Mitch. *Understanding September 11th: Answering Questions about the Attacks on America*. New York: Scholastic, 2002. Print.

Schier, Helga. *September 11, 2001*. Edina, MN: ABDO, 2008. Print.

Thoms, Annie. *With Their Eyes: September 11th—The View from a High School at Ground Zero*. New York: HarperCollins, 2002. Print.

Web Links

To learn more about the capture and killing of Osama bin Laden, visit ABDO Publishing Company online at **www.abdopublishing. com**. Web sites about the capture and killing of Osama bin Laden are featured on our Book Links page. These links are routinely monitored and updated to provide the most current information available.

Places to Visit

Flight 93 National Memorial
Shanksville, PA
www.nps.gov/flni/index.htm
The dedication of this site honoring the victims of UA flight 93 was scheduled for September 11, 2011. The first phase of construction was finished in 2011, and the completed monument will include a memorial plaza, field of honor, and visitors facilities.

**National September 11 Memorial & Museum
at the World Trade Center**
One Liberty Plaza, 20th Floor
New York, NY 10006
212-312-8800
www.911memorial.org
This memorial was scheduled to be dedicated on September 11, 2011 and open to the public on September 12. The memorial remembers those who died in the 9/11 attacks with a museum and park.

Pentagon Memorial
1 Rotary Road
Washington, DC 20301-1155
www.whs.mil/memorial
The Pentagon Memorial is dedicated to those who died in the 9/11 attacks on the Pentagon. This memorial site includes an American Heroes memorial and chapel, as well as 184 illuminated outdoor benches, one for each person who died in the attack.

SOURCE NOTES

Chapter 1. September 11, 2001

1. "The Flight 93 Story." *Flight 93 National Memorial*. National Parks Service, US Department of the Interior, 19 June 2011. Web. 7 July 2011.

2. Roger Simon. "Blown Away." *U.S. News & World Report*. usnews. com, 9 Sept. 2001. Web. 7 July 2011.

3. "Day of Infamy: A Timeline of Terror." *U.S. News & World Report*. usnews.com, 9 Sept. 2001. Web. 7 July 2011.

4. "The End of Bin Laden." *Time* magazine. 20 May 2011: 46. Print.

5. "The End of Bin Laden." *Time* magazine. 20 May 2011: 46. Print.

6. "Obama's Remarks on Bin Laden's Killing." *New York Times*. New York Times, 2 2011. Web. 7 July 2011.

Chapter 2. A History of Terrorism

1. "What Is Terrorism?" *International Terrorism and Security Research*. Terrorism-Research.com, n.d. Web. 7 July 2011.

2. "President William McKinley: Assassinated by an Anarchist." *Historynet.com*. Weider History Group, 12 June 2006. Web. 7 July 2011.

3. Adam Roberts. "The Changing Faces of Terrorism." *BBC*. BBC, 27 Aug. 2002. Web. 7 July 2011.

4. "FBI 100: First Strike: Global Terror in America." *Federal Bureau of Investigation*. US Department of Justice, 26 Feb. 2008. Web. 7 July 2011.

5. David C. Rapoport. "The Four Waves of Modern Terrorism." In Audrey Cronin and J. Ludes (eds). *Attacking Terrorism: Elements of a Grand Strategy*. Washington, DC: Georgetown UP, 2004. 61.

Chapter 3. Who Was Osama bin Laden?

1. Peter Bergen. "A Long Time Going." *Time* magazine. Time, 20 May 2011. Web. 7 July 2011.

2. Steve Coll. "Letter from Jedda: Young Osama." *The New Yorker*. New Yorker, 12 Dec. 2005. Web. 7 July 2011.

3. Ibid.

4. Ibid.

5. "A Biography of Osama bin Laden." *Frontline*. WGBH, 1999. Web. 7 July 2011.

Chapter 4. Defender of Islam

1. "Bin Laden's Fatwa." *PBS NewsHour*. MacNeil/Lehrer Productions, Aug. 1996. Web. 7 July 2011.

2. "Bin Laden's Murderous 1998 'Fatwa': 'Comply With God's Order to Kill the Americans.'" *CNSNEWs.com*. Cybercast News Service, 2 May 2011. Web. 7 July 2011.

3. Shaykh Hisham Kabbani and Shaykh Seraj Hendricks. "Jihad—A Misunderstood Concept from Islam." *sunnah.org*. As-Sunnah Foundation, n.d. Web. 7 July 2011.

4. Rahimullah Yusufzai. "Conversation with Terror." *Time* magazine. Time, 11 Jan. 1999. Web. 7 July 2011.

5. "Suspect 'Reveals 9/11 Planning,'" *BBC*. BBC, 22 Sept. 2003. Web. 7 July 2011.

6. "Missed Opportunities: The CIA and bin Laden." *ABC News*. ABCNews.com, 10 Sept. 2006. Web. 7 July 2011.

Chapter 5. The United States Fights Back

1. "Text: Bin Laden's Statement." *Guardian.co.uk*. Guardian News and Media, 7 Oct. 2001. Web. 7 July 2011.

2. "President Bush's Speech." *Online NewsHour*. MacNeil/Lehrer Productions, 7 Oct. 2001. Web. 7 July 2011.

3. Philip Smucker. "How bin Laden Got Away." *Christian Science Monitor*. Christian Science Monitor, 4 Mar. 2002. Web. 7 July 2011.

4. Mary Anne Weaver. "Lost at Tora Bora." *New York Times*. New York Times, 11 Sept. 2005. Web. 7 July 2011.

5. Ibid.

6. Raymond Ibrahim, ed. *The Al-Qaeda Reader*. New York: Doubleday, 2007. *Google Book Search*. Web. 7 July 2011.

7. Tricia McDermott. "Transcript: Bush's 9/11 Remarks." *CBS News*. CBSNews.com, 11 Sept. 2006. Web. 7 July 2011.

Source Notes Continued

Chapter 6. The Hunt Is On

1. Associated Press. "CIA Reportedly Disbands Bin Laden Unit." *Washington Post*. Washington Post, 4 July 2006. Web. 7 July 2011.

2. Karen de Young. "Letter Gives Glimpse of Al-Qaeda's Leadership." *Washington Post*. Washington Post, 2 Oct. 2006. Web. 7 July 2011.

3. "On Tape, bin Laden Mourns al-Zarqawi's Death." *CNN*. Cable News Network, 30 June 2006. Web. 7 July 2011.

4. Lisa Meyers. "An Interview with a Taliban Commander." *NBC Nightly News*. MSNBC.com, 27 Dec. 2005. Web. 7 July 2011.

5. Peter Bergen. "Trees and Tapes May Hint at bin Laden Location." *CNN*. Cable News Network, 23 Aug. 2006. Web. 7 July 2011.

6. George Stephanopoulos. "Where Is bin Laden? Secretary Gates Says No Intel in 'Years.'" *ABC News*. ABCNews.com, 5 Dec. 2009. Web. 7 July 2011.

Chapter 7. "We Will Kill bin Laden"

1. Kelly Arena. "Obama Administration to Ratchet Up Hunt for bin Laden." *CNN*. Cable News Network, 12 Nov. 2008. Web. 7 July 2011.

2. Tom Baldwin. "Barack Obama: It Is No Longer Essential to Kill Osama bin Laden." *Times*. Times Newspapers, 5 Jan. 2009. Web. 7 July 2011.

3. Mark Colvin. "I Was bin Laden's Bodyguard." *ABC.net.au*. Australian Broadcasting Company, 29 Apr. 2010. Web. 7 July 2011.

4. Barbara Starr. "NATO Official: Bin Laden, Deputy Hiding in Northwest Pakistan." *CNN*. Cable News Network, 18 Oct. 2010. Web. 7 July 2011.

5. "Highlights: Key Points in the Raid that Killed bin Laden." *CNN*. Cable News Network, 5 May 2011. Web. 7 July 2011.

6. Elisabeth Bumiller, Carlotta Gall and Salman Masood. "Bin Laden's Secret Life in a Diminished World." *New York Times*. New York Times, 7 May 2011. Web. 7 July 2011.

7. Greg Miller. "CIA Spied on bin Laden from Safe House." *Washington Post*. Washington Post, 5 May 2011. Web. 7 July 2011.

Chapter 8. "We Got Him"

1. David Von Drehle. "Death Comes for the Terrorist." *Time* magazine. 20 May 2011: 16. Print.

2. Ibid. 19.

3. David Von Drehle. "Death Comes for the Terrorist." *Time* magazine. 20 May 2011: 19. Print.

4. Christopher Dickey. "A Decade on the Lam." *Newsweek*. Newsweek/Daily Beast, 5 May 2011. Web. 7 July 2011.

5. David Von Drehle. "Death Comes for the Terrorist." *Time* magazine. 20 May 2011: 26. Print.

6. Tom A. Peter. "Somalia Kills Fazul Abdullah Mohammed, Widening Al Qaeda Power Vacuum." *Christian Science Monitor*. Christian Science Monitor, 12 June 2011. Web. 7 July 2011.

7. David Von Drehle. "Death Comes for the Terrorist." *Time* magazine. 20 May 2011: 26. Print.

Chapter 9. The World Reacts

1. Macon Phillips. "Osama bin Laden Dead." *White House Blog*. www.whitehouse.gov, 2 May 2011. Web. 7 July 2011.

2. "Bush, Victims, World Leaders React to bin Laden's Death." *MSNBC.com*. MSNBC, 2 May 2011. Web. 7 July 2011.

3. Kayla Webley. "Crowds, Chaos and Some Closure and Ground Zero." *Time* magazine. Time, 2 May 2011. Web. 7 July 2011.

4. Ibid.

5. David Von Drehle. "Death Comes for the Terrorist." *Time Magazine*. 20 May 2011: 28. Print.

6. "Osama bin Laden's Death: Aftermath and Reaction— Wednesday 4 May 2011." *Guardian.co.uk*. Guardian News and Media, 4 May 2011. Web. 7 July 2011.

7. Philip Ittner. "Pakistan Stunned by bin Laden's Death." *VOA News*. VOAnews.com, 2 May 2011. Web. 7 July 2011.

8. Brian Montopoli. "Obama: I Won't Release bin Laden Death Photos." *CBS News*. CBSNews.com, 4 May 2011. Web. 7 July 2011.

9. Fareed Zakaria. "When Terror Loses Its Grip." *Time* magazine. 20 May 2011: 51. Print.

10. "Al-Qaeda Leader Ayman al-Zawahiri Vows to Avenge Osama bin Laden's Death." *Telegraph*. Telegraph Media Group, 25 June 2011. Web. 7 July 2011.

INDEX

ABOUT THE AUTHOR

Marcia Amidon Lusted is the author of 60 books for young people, as well as hundreds of magazine articles. She is an assistant editor, a musician, and a writing instructor.

PHOTO CREDITS

AP Images, cover, 3, 55; Jim Collins/AP Images, 6, 99 (top); Doug Mills/AP Images, 10; Al Jazeera/AP Images, 13; Antonia Tozer/ John Warburton-Lee Photography/Photolibrary, 14; Eric Isselée/ Shutterstock Images, 16; The Daily Oklahoman/Jim Argo/AP Images, 20; Jacques Langevin/AP Images, 25, 97; iStockphoto, 26, 96 (top); US Army/AP Images, 31; AFP/AFP/Getty Images, 35, 96 (bottom); Keith Bernstein/Getty Images, 36; Haider Shah/ AP Images, 40; Al-Jazeera/APTN/AP Images, 42; Tom Horan/ AP Images, 45; Win McNamee/AP Images, 46; US Department of Defense, 50, 56, 98; U.S. Department of State/HO/AP Images, 59; US Navy, 63; Mark Wilson/AP Images, 65; Pablo Martinez Monsivais/AP Images, 66; Kiloran Howard/Photolibrary, 69; Red Line Editorial, 73; The White House/Pete Souza/AP Images, 74; Anjum Naveed/AP Images, 77; CIA/AP Images, 80; Lenny Ignelzi/ AP Images, 83, 99 (bottom); Jason DeCrow/AP Images, 84; Asianet-Pakistan/Shutterstock Images, 88; Time/AP Images, 95